# ColourScene
## Snapshot

# ALDENHAM
## and
# CHISWICK

## N. J. Eadon-Clarke

DTS
Publishing

ISBN: 1-900515-36-9

© 2006  N. J. Eadon-Clarke

Published by: DTS Publishing  PO Box 105, Croydon CR9 2TL  *www.dtspublishing.co.uk*

Printed by: Ian Allan Printing Limited

British Library Cataloguing in Publication Data. A catalogue record for this book is available from the British Library

**FRONT COVER:** The overhauled body from RM363 is being gently lowered onto overhauled sub frames, the employees are making fina checks of the attachment points and it will then move to the paint shop and gain a new identity. **21 July 1977**

**BACK COVER:** RT1615 performing on the world famous Chiswick works skid pan. The bus carries a board saying "skid bus" in the fron nearside window. The final photo shows how a London bus driver is expected to end with the bus perfectly positioned. Note the passengers enjoying the experience seated on the lower deck. **29 July 1976**

# Foreword

This is the first of a new series of 'ColourScene Snapshot' books which will each focus on a particular subject and illustrate the scene on specific dates.

The London Transport bus works at Chiswick and Aldenham held a particular fascination for any bus enthusiast and the opportunity to step inside the gates to see their inner workings was something not to be missed. In the 1970s London Transport organised a series of summer tours to its major establishments (road, rail and other supporting establishments such as the ticket machine works and signal training schools) for which one could apply for tickets. I was successful in gaining tickets to visit Aldenham Bus Overhaul Works in 1972 and 1977 and Chiswick Works in 1973 and 1976, In addition London Transport held public open days at Aldenham in 1979 and 1983 and at Chiswick in 1983 and 1984. This book contains a selection of photographs taken during those visits which show the various activities that went into supporting the buses of London.

I wish to thank Keith Hamer for providing the general information on Aldenham Bus Overhaul works which I have had to shorten to fit the space available and for other comments which I have incorporated where possible; any remaining errors are mine. I am very grateful to Mike Davis of DTS Publishing who has kindly put the book together to meet my vision and undertaken all the other arrangements to allow the book to reach the bookshelves.

Now that both establishments have closed I hope you find this collection of photographs will bring back memories of a bygone era in bus maintenance.

Nigel Eadon-Clarke                                                              July 2006
Chislehurst
Kent
UK

# ALDENHAM BUS OVERHAUL WORKS

Aldenham bus overhaul works occupied a 67 acre site and was first designated for railway use in 1864. In 1937 it was proposed to build an Underground Maintenance depot and sidings on the site for a proposed extension of the Northern Line from Edgware to Bushey Heath.

Although a war situation was looming construction work began in summer 1939 and the main workshops were completed by the summer of 1940 before work ceased so that the labour and materials could be transferred to the war effort.

It would have been a waste not to utilise these new buildings, and being so near to both Leavesden and Radlett Aerodrome's, Government approval was obtained to use the new buildings for the construction of aircraft for the RAF. Chiswick Works was already building aircraft in association with the Ministry of Aviation and the London Aircraft Construction Group, and in 1941 LT further extended this unison by transferring staff to urgently build the Halifax bomber, Mosquito fuselages and aircraft engines.

After the war the Northern Line extension was officially abandoned. LT decided to keep the premises, as Chiswick works was full to overflowing, and a new bus overhaul works was urgently required for the 'standardised' new post-war fleet. Much had been learnt from the aircraft assembly, notably the efficient use of parts manufacture and the structure of designated work areas.

The re-construction of the site slowly continued between 1952-54, the largest of the carriage sheds became the main area for the lifting of bus bodies, overhead cranes being installed over the length of the building, under which would accommodate over 100 buses.

Although it had been used for some time the 'official' opening of the works took place on 30th October 1956 and it was christened 'London Transport Aldenham Bus Overhaul Works'. The name derives from the adjoining Aldenham reservoir, as Aldenham village is some distance away.

There was a standardised fleet strength of some 7,700 buses. Each bus was overhauled and repainted every 3-4 years, which resulted in an average weekly output from Aldenham of some 40 buses (the works was built with an expectation to overhaul up to 10,000 buses at 56 per week) making it the largest bus works in the world.

Aldenham operated something called a 'works float' which was first set up for the overhauling of the RT group of buses, this was an authorised system of reducing costs on vehicle excise duty (road tax), as each bus would be off the road for at least 4-6 weeks. This followed the body removal system that had been successfully employed at Chiswick for decades. Chassis units were normally ready weeks before the body, major mechanical units being sent and returned to Chiswick by lorry. The float put vehicles back on the road quicker without the need to await their original bodies. Buses placed on the 'float' would effectively be delicensed, and that stock number removed until relicensing again, which with some RTs lasted some 12 years. The 100 or so chassis-less bodies constantly being

worked upon were therefore the unlicensed 'works float' in real terms.

It was not that unusual for a ferry driver to deliver the same 'stock number' to and from the works. For example, a newly overhauled bus, say RML2590 (which spent its entire life at Putney Garage), would be delivered to the garage from the works, and another RML2590 would be picked up for return, the ferry driver using trade plates, the tax disk being transferred from old to new at the garage. An observant passenger on route 14 could well have travelled on RML2590 one day, and travelled on a sparkling overhauled RML2590 the next day, wondering how that effect could have been achieved overnight! Of course they are two different vehicles, with different chassis and bodies, albeit carrying the same stock and registration number.

In 1978 the large DMS class became due for overhaul; it was deemed prohibitively costly to separate body and chassis so a large part of the floor space at the works was set aside for these overhauls.

Aldenham was of course also famous for its fleet of staff buses, mainly time expired buses that still had some life left. RTLs and RTWs were replaced by RTs and a couple of GSs, and these were later replaced by RMAs. As time progressed and as more staff were recruited far and wide, so staff buses could be seen going as far afield as Aylesbury and Luton.

Buses gradually became more robust and increased certificates of fitness meant buses could last seven years without overhaul, but it was proved they could not go that long without a repaint. Therefore a mid-term repaint became standard, and Aldenham began a separate programme of repaints from March 1967 and even after the formation of LCBS on 1/1/70 continued to carry out work on behalf of LCBS until their own facilities became available.

The works in full swing was a mighty impressive sight, with the overhead cranes lifting bodies in the main workshop where a line of some 50-plus buses were always being worked upon (2 lines when opened!), the repaint area, and the heavy accident repair workshop for seriously damaged buses. Aldenham of course had many other smaller departments, the manufacture of blinds, woodwork and metal assembly, seat-trim shops, the famous tilt-test, and the licensing department. All were gradually reduced or re-allocated as input dropped.

The works passed its ownership to Bus Engineering Ltd from 1st April 1985, but it was already in decline. The introduction of yearly Freedom From Defect tests from 1982 and other changes at garages meant that the majority of work could be carried out in garages, and some major overhauls were being contracted to outside bodies. The works finally closed on 15th November 1986 and the vast buildings remained empty for years, until being completely demolished and cleared in 1997, to form what is today the Centenniel Park Industrial Estate.

**ABOVE and BELOW:** A green RML from LCBS has arrived in the initial inspection area, in the picture above to the right are the Routemaster sub frames from which a body has already been separated. In the picture below those sub frames have been wheeled away and the body on the RML is being lifted from its sub frames under close supervision. **24 August 1972**

**ABOVE:** Blue Arrow liveried LCBS XF7 has arrived in the body shop for refurbishment and repainting back to green following the ending of the Blue Arrow service in Stevenage. **24 August 1972**

**BELOW:** Routemaster bodies in the body shop for attention having been separated from their chassis and delivered to this area via overhead crane visible in the background. **24 August 1972**

**ABOVE:** A green LCBS RML with new panels and having been re-united with a chassis is being towed to the paint shop. **24 August 1972**

**BELOW:** This is MBA 606 which has received an undercoat in preparation to receive the overall advertisement livery for Chappel's music store. **24 August 1972**

**ABOVE:** Former Blue Arrow LCBS XF8 stands amongst an RM, RT and RF awaiting finishing touches before being repainted green, **24 August 1972**

**BELOW:** General view of the paint preparation area showing many different types of vehicle. **24 August 1972**

**ABOVE:** MB645 has received a coat of red paint and is being inspected before the next stage of the paint process. **24 August 1972**

**BELOW:** RT1890 is about to enter another painting booth, close inspection reveals the front wheels are clear of the ground, the bus will be moved via cables set into the floor. **24 August 1972**

**ABOVE:** Heavy accident victims requiring repairs beyond the scope of local garage repairs were dealt with by Aldenham works. Here a New Cross based DMS requires frontal repair. **24 August 1972**

**BELOW:** Sunlight shines through the roof of the works as LCBS RC3 is seen shortly after repainting into green livery. **24 August 1972**

**ABOVE:** RM722 has just been repainted and is receiving fleet transfers and finishing touches. **24 August 1972**

**BELOW:** RT4688 is just emerging from the hot spraying booth, the cables attached to the underside of the bus can be clearly seen. **24 August 1972**

**ABOVE:** Unfortunately this photograph is overexposed, but it demonstrates the tilt test being undertaken by RM703. **24 August 1972**

**BELOW:** The front parking area of Aldenham works used by vehicles bringing employees from all over London. Here the Abbey Wood staff bus GS13 stands between RTs. **24 August 1972**

**ABOVE:** Brand new vehicles were delivered to Aldenham, it being conveniently near both the M1 motorway and the A41 trunk road. Here 4 new DMS fleetlines await final inspection. They are from the 44x, 45x batch bodied by Park Royal and the 13xx batch bodied by Metro-Cammell. **24 August 1972**

**BELOW:** New DMS fleetlines from the 13xx batch bodied by Metro-Cammell stand in the front yard. **24 August 1972**

**ABOVE:** More new DMSs mostly from the 45x batch bodied by Park Royal vehicles stand in the front yard. **24 August 1972**

**BELOW**: New DMS1300 stands amongst others of the class in the front yard at Aldenham works. **24 August 1972**

**ABOVE:** The two Routemaster sub frames bolted together to allow easy movement within the workshops have just received silver paint. **21 July 1977**

**BELOW:** Body repairs have been completed on former RM363. It is being transported by overhead crane to be re-united with sub frames whereupon it will gain a new identity. **21 July 1977**

**ABOVE and BELOW:** The overhauled body from RM363 is being gently lowered onto overhauled sub frames, the employees are making final checks of the attachment points and it will then move to the paint shop and gain a new identity. **21 July 1977**

**ABOVE:** The body from RM48 from Sidcup garage has been placed on this inverter and turned through 90° to allow the underside to be cleaned and repaired. The high pressure hose used for cleaning can be seen in action. **21 July 1977**

**BELOW:** The body from RM1989 of Dalston garage is being moved by a trolley within the repair area. **21 July 1977**

**ABOVE:** Inside the accident repair shop we find a couple of Metropolitans and DMSs 101, 220 and 1991. **21 July 1977**

**BELOW:** SM23 is in the process of being re-certified and is receiving body panel repair. The yellow clamps on the wheels will allow the complete bus to be lifted. **21 July 1977**

6029: SM19 is also being re-certified for further use. 21 July 1977

6030: BS12 from Enfield garage is receiving repairs after a heavy accident. 21 July 1977

6031: Routemasters in the works for attention. Here RML901 stands next to British Airways No.6. 21 July 1977

6032: Completed RM237 stands on the weighbridge to check all is well. 21 July 1977

**ABOVE:** A Walthamstow based DMS (believed to be 1528) is being repaired following an engine fire. **21 July 1977**

**BELOW:** The back part of Aldenham works had been leased to British Leyland, but was returned to LT who needed it to cope with Swift and Fleetline overhaul because the bodies could not be removed from their chassis requiring more space. Here SMS186 from Bromley garage is being prepared for re-certification. **21 July 1977**

**ABOVE:** Next to SMS186 we find a gleaming SM41complete with the new 'solid' London Transport roundel. **21 July 1977**

**BELOW:** Two DMSs in the works for modification. On the left is DMS2200 which was used as a farebox float vehicle and next to it is DMS1673 which had been a training bus at Sidcup garage. **21 July 1977**

**ABOVE:** Raised by wheel hoists is SMS200 in the course of being re-certified. **21 July 1977**

**BELOW:** Two Routemaster sub frames are seen here bolted together by the silver joining plates to allow the combined units to proceed to the chassis cleaning area. **21 July 1977**

**ABOVE:** The painting preparation area sees a Routemaster with rubbed down paint and new panels being readied for spray painting. **21 July 1977**

**BELOW:** RM285 has just emerged from the hot spray painting area, it will have transfers applied before varnishing. A small black trolley can be seen behind the bus to which buses are attached to allow movement through the spray booths. **21 July 1977**

**ABOVE:** An unidentified SMS is being prepared for painting, note that the windscreen is covered with cream rather than paper or a masking plate. The windscreen wipers, lights and mirrors are covered by masking tape. **21 July 1977**

**LEFT:** This is DMS799 being prepared for spray painting in a similar way to the SMS shown previously. **21 July 1977**

**ABOVE:** Emerging from hot varnish spraying is RML2705. **21 July 1977**

**BELOW:** Two brand new buses near the paint line in the works where they have been fitted with transfers. B20 type DMSs 2452 and 2449. **21 July 1977**

**ABOVE:** SM38 has been repainted and is just awaiting final inspection and finishing touches by hand. **21 July 1977**

**BELOW:** This is the licensing shop where the bus will receive its final MOT checks before being issued with a licence to operate again. Here RM715 is awaiting final clearance. **21 July 1977**

**ABOVE:** Just outside the licensing shop we find a stark contrast between new B20 DMS2426 and a 'tatty' looking RT1665 which is the Harrow Weald staff bus. **21 July 1977**

**BELOW:** Completed and ready to leave is SMS160 seen outside the licensing shop. **21 July 1977**

**ABOVE:** Brand new vehicles parked in the front yard DMS2461 has a body built by Park Royal, similar DMS2252 is bodied by MCW and finally LS94 from Leyland at Workington. **21 July 1977**

**BELOW:** These two SMDs have been relegated to staff bus duties. SMD435 has brought employees from New Cross garage and SMD438 from Plumstead garage. **21 July 1977**

**ABOVE:** Brand new Park Royal bodied DMSs 2465 and 2466 stand in the front yard. **21 July 1977**

**BELOW:** Aldenham works open day and new vehicles stand in the front yard, from left to right are LSs 384, 378, 368, 354 & 381, Ms 104, 112, 96 and 100. **16 September 1979**

**ABOVE:** In the pre-inspection area we see RM1362 and DMS387 both of which have arrived for overhaul. **16 September 1979**

**BELOW:** Routemaster sub frames with the clearly visible rear coil springs outside the chassis washing booth. **16 September 1979**

**ABOVE:** DMS383 during the course of its overhaul; because it proved impracticable to separate the body and chassis on DMS fleetlines the vehicle was overhauled complete by means of wheel hoists as seen here. This meant that the complete vehicle would be 'off the road' for weeks, sometimes months unlike the system used previously for RT and RM vehicles which by means of the body 'float' system allowed a vehicle with the same stock number to return to service within one week. **16 September 1979**

**BELOW:** An unidentified Routemaster in the paint preparation shop. **16 September 1979**

**ABOVE:** General view of the paintshop preparation area (and many visitors) during the open day. **16 September 1979**

**LEFT:** Routemaster sub frames in the chassis painting booth. **16 September 1979**

CHASSIS PAINT

**ABOVE:** The vehicle with 'no front' is RM545 obviously in the workshop following an extremely heavy accident. **16 September 1979**

**BELOW:** Demonstrating the method of moving bodies separated from their sub frames is a Routemaster body being transported by overhead crane to the body repair area. **16 September 1979**

**ABOVE:** This is DMS2236 from Catford garage in the accident repair shop. **16 September 1979**

**BELOW:** RML2321 was one of the three RMLs received from London Country Bus Services in exchange for the three XAs it is seen here undergoing body repairs as part of its overhaul. **16 September 1979**

**ABOVE**: MBA611 being prepared for overhaul. **16 September 1979**

**BELOW:** Although DMS Fleetlines were not separated from their chassis during overhaul they still required to be inverted to allow chassis cleaning and repair, DMS390 demonstrates this process. **16 September 1979**

**ABOVE:** Watched by many visitors the body of RML2298 (body number B2363) is lifted clear of the sub frames in the body dismount area. The body and sub frames will be overhauled separately and it was extremely rare for a body to be reunited with its original chassis on completion. This was because body repairs take longer that chassis repairs. LT employed a system whereby identities were changed to allow a vehicle with the same stock number to be returned to service within a few days, but in reality this would be a different vehicle. (see photograph on page 41, taken on the same day of another vehicle numbered RML2298 ready to leave the works). **16 September 1979**

**BELOW:** In the body dismount area awaiting separation we see on the left RML2395 and next to it RM1394. **16 September 1979**

**ABOVE:** This is open top convertible DMO7 used on the Round London Sightseeing tour. Alongside can be seen its demountable roof. **16 September 1979**

**BELOW:** In the accident repair shop we see DM975 which has received extensive frontal damage. **16 September 1979**

**ABOVE:** During the open day this part of the works remained cordoned off to visitors; nevertheless we can note new Metrobuses M99, 101 and 102. At the back is DM1757 which hit the headlines at the time after its low bridge accident. **16 September 1979**

**LEFT:** An unidentified Routemaster in the spray paint booth. **16 September 1979**

**ABOVE:** This unidentified DM has just been spray painted and awaits hot varnishing. **16 September 1979**

**BELOW:** This RML has been painted and awaits hot varnishing. **16 September 1979**

**ABOVE:** Apprentices at Aldenham work would carry out work on vehicles from the London Transport Museum collection. Seen here for painting are Trolleybus 1253 and LT165. **16 September 1979**

**BELOW:** Aldenham works also manufactured blind displays as shown here in the blind shop. This being an example for Southall garage vehicles. **16 September 1979**

**ABOVE:** RM1913 has just emerged from the hot varnish booth. Of note is that it carries an incorrect registration, it should read ALD913B. It will no doubt be corrected before leaving the works. **16 September 1979**

**LEFT:** Here is RML2298 (body B2378) ready to leave the works (see photograph on page 36 of another RML2298 on the same day entering the works). **16 September 1979**

**ABOVE:** RM1414 is receiving its final checks in the licensing shop to allow it to return to passenger service. This bus would later pass to the Manchester Museum of Transport and is pictured again later in this book (on 5 Aug 84). **16 September 1979**

**BELOW:** Also in the licensing shop for final checks is RM1394. **16 September 1979**

**ABOVE:** Brand new Metrobus M97 is also receiving its final inspection in the licensing shop. **16 September 1979**

**BELOW:** Brand new Leyland Titans including Ts 42, 56, 48 & 64 parked outside the works awaiting entry into service, note the application of 'multi ride' stickers on the front for operation from Romford (North Street) garage. **16 September 1979**

**ABOVE:** Also awaiting entry into service is new Metrobus M95, visible behind is SMD96. **16 September 1979**

**BELOW:** Severely accident damaged SMS328 is awaiting its fate at the works. **16 September 1979**

**ABOVE:** New Metrobus M90 worked on the free bus service between the works and Stanmore station during this open day seen here about to leave the works. **16 September 1979**

**BELOW:** Also operating on the free service to Stanmore station was Leyland Titan T46. **16 September 1979**

**ABOVE:** Recently overhauled RM1232 passes Metrobus M92 outside the works. **16 September 1979**

**BELOW:** A general view of the works with preserved RLH29 attending for the open day on its way out. **16 September 1979**

**ABOVE:** Also leaving the works is a new Metrobus on its way to Stanmore station. **16 September 1979**

**BELOW:** And a new Leyland Titan leaves for Stanmore station. **16 September 1979**

**ABOVE:** Brand new Leyland Nationals parked in the front yard awaiting entry into service, from left to right we have LSs 372, 373, 379, 384 and 378. **16 September 1979**

**BELOW:** Leyland Titan T286 under overhaul seen inside the works during the second general open day. **25 September 1983**

**LEFT:** D2626 being prepared for repainting inside the works. **25 September 1983**

**BELOW:** D2623 is also being prepared for repainting. **25 September 1983**

**ABOVE:** DMS2474 is seen on the paint line having received red paint it now awaits hot varnish. **25 September 1983**

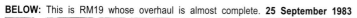

**BELOW:** This is RM19 whose overhaul is almost complete. **25 September 1983**

**ABOVE:** RMC1464 heads a convoy of training RMCs outside the workshops. **25 September 1983**

**BELOW:** These are the remains of LCBS DL6 seen in the Leyland centre adjacent to Aldenham works. **25 September 1983**

**ABOVE:** Fire vicitim LS401 from Bromley garage seen awaiting assessment as to its future. It survived and still operates in 2006 in the ownership of Metro Business Aviation at Stansted Airport. **25 September 1983**

**BELOW:** Newly painted Leyland Titans T112 and T113 are parked in the front yard to demonstrate the new 'express' livery for vehicles to work on Route 177 Express. **25 September 1983**

**ABOVE:** In an effort to sell members of the Metropolitan class MD127 has been painted in this unique livery to attract potential buyers, note the blind display shows "one careful owner". **25 September 1983**

**BELOW:** Immaculately restored RM855 was working the free service to Stanmore station. The blind display refers to the 50th anniversary since the formation of London Transport in 1933. Close observation will also reveal that this is an early body (body B293) since in addition to opening upper front windows it retains the vents above these windows to provide internal upper deck ventilation prior to the decision to fit opening front upper windows. Of particular interest is that a photograph of this bus taken at this event was used on one of the internal posters adorning the last Routemasters on route 159 to represent the Routemaster in the 1980s. **25 September 1983**

# CHISWICK WORKS

Chiswick works opened in 1921 and occupied a 32 acre site set up by the London General Omnibus Company to maintain their bus fleet and also to build new bodies for buses. From the outset an important function was the overhaul of mechanical units and the supply of reconditioned units to the various garages by lorry. In later years Aldenham was also a main recipient of these units.

With a war situation looming Chiswick began planning and as bus work decreased work switched to supporting the war effort which included work on Merlin engines for the RAF and work on armoured vehicles. Together with Aldenham Chiswick was part of the London Aircraft Production Group and produced components for the Halifax bomber and engineering lessons learnt would be applied to bus work after the war.

Other departments at Chiswick included the experimental department which was expanded in 1937 and the world famous training school and Skid Pan. This utilised a special surface that was sprayed with water and all drivers were expected to bring a skidding bus under control before being allowed to drive buses in London passenger service.

After the war London Transport found itself with a large and expanding fleet and a review of the capacity at Chiswick was undertaken resulting in the chassis line and some other functions being moved to Aldenham although overhaul of all mechanical units remained the responsibility of Chiswick.

In the 80s the era of bus operators maintaining large centralised overhaul works was drawing to a close. Buses were more reliable and overhaul no longer required the separation of the body from the chassis. More work was being undertaken at garages or by outside contractors. When Aldenham closed some work was transferred back to Chiswick which was now being operated by Bus Engineering Ltd set up to manage LT's Engineering. In spring 1987 BEL was taken over by Frontsource Ltd, but operation of the site became increasing unviable and it closed in spring 1990. The site has now been redeveloped as a prestigious business park under the name of 'Chiswick Park'.

**BELOW:** This view outside the Chiswick works experimental shop shows SMS100 which despite being delivered in May 1970 had yet to enter passenger service it having spent its whole life to date at Chiswick. **2 August 1973**

**LEFT:** RM2 seen outside the Chiswick experimental shop. **2 August 1973**

**BELOW:** Also allocated to the Chiswick experimental shop were DMS660 and RM2 as seen here in this slightly overexposed photograph. **2 August 1973**

**LEFT:** LT had acquired a batch of six Leyland Nationals for trials on route S2. Subsequently a batch of 51 originally intended for Venezuela was diverted to LT and would be used at Hounslow garage. The first of these LS7 was delivered in May 1976 and is seen here leaving Chiswick works on a training run. **29 July 1976**

# The Chiswick Skid Pan

These four views show RT1615 performing on the world famous Chiswick works skid pan. The bus carries a board saying "skid bus" in the front nearside window. The final photo shows how a London bus driver is expected to end with the bus perfectly positioned. Note the passengers enjoying the experience seated on the lower deck. **29 July 1976**

**ABOVE:** General view of the bus parking area alongside the skid pan. BL4 is at the front, also visible are various RTs RMs and an RF in the corner. **29 July 1976**

**BELOW:** New Leyland National LS7 is undergoing road trials and in this view is passing the skid pan. **29 July 1976**

**ABOVE:** LT converted four BEA 1½ deck AEC Regal coaches into uniform issue buses that would tour each garage on a regular basis. Here former BEA MLL727 is seen inside Chiswick works with a new stock number (1466W) in the service vehicle fleet. **29 July 1976**

**BELOW:** MB182 was specially overhauled in an effort to attract potential overseas buyers for the class. Looking like new it stands here in the grounds of Chiswick works. **29 July 1976**

**ABOVE:** General view of the famous Chiswick 'dip' with an RT heading the line of parked buses. If you look closely at the back you can see the rear of new Leyland National LS40 parked in the experimental shop. **29 July 1976**

**BELOW:** General view of the Chiswick works training bus park , amongst various RTs can be seen BL4 and LS7, the BL is officially allocated to Romford (North Street) garage for training purposes. **29 July 1976**

**ABOVE:** The training park contains representatives of the various classes a new driver was likely to encounter, here we find MB312, DMS393, MD30 together with assorted RMs and RTs. **29 July 1976**

**BELOW:** The four vehicles at the front of the training park are RT2167, RT684, RML898 and RM641. **29 July 1976**

**ABOVE:** A closer view of MB312 (and interested visitor with notebook) in the training park. **29 July 1976**

**BELOW:** A fine line up of vehicles in the Chiswick Works training park, from left to right RTs 2059, 3680, 3828 & 710 together with RM528. **29 July 1976**

**ABOVE:** RML898 and RM641 stand between duties in the training park. **29 July 1976**

**BELOW:** Smartly turned out DMS393 and MD30 also in the training park. **29 July 1976**

**ABOVE:** The proud driver of new BL4 has stopped the vehicle for this photograph. **29 July 1976**

**BELOW:** Seen at the back of the training park is RF491 alongside RM853. **29 July 1976**

**ABOVE:** RM1 seen outside the Chiswick experimental shop. **29 July 1976**
**BELOW:** RM1368 had suffered a fire to its top deck, it was subsequently converted into this single deck form and thereby allowed the experimental shop to release RM8 for passenger service. RM1368 is now privately preserved in this form. **29 July 1976**

**ABOVE:** RM2 was painted into this silver livery to allow potential advertisers to view the look prior to the painting of 25 Routemasters into a similar silver livery the following year to celebrate the Queen's silver jubilee in 1977, seen here outside the experimental shop. **29 July 1976**

**BELOW:** Chiswick works held a Jubilee Gala in 1983, here works ambulance 1532B is seen outside the works surgery. **2 July 1983**

66

**ABOVE:** RM1933 has been painted into this smart '1933' livery for the 50th anniversary of London Transport. It stands next to 'Showbus' RM1737. **2 July 1983**

**BELOW:** The driver of RT1530 shows-off his skills whilst passengers board RMC1518 (right background) for hair-raising rides across the skid pan, as depicted on the following two pages. **2 July 1983**

# RMC1518 on the Skid Pan

These four photographs show RMC1518 performing on the world famous skid pan taken from outside and inside the bus, visitors were allowed to travel in the downstairs saloon only. **2 July 1983**

**ABOVE:** Another view of RT1530 on the skid pan, with T681 in the background. **2 July 1983**

**BELOW:** At one time it had been expected that RT1599 would operate the last RT passenger journey and it had been spruced up accordingly. In the event it performed on the last day of RTs on route 140 from Harrow Weald garage, but RTs soldiered on for longer at Barking garage. Here the RT looks lonely in the training park. **2 July 1983**

**ABOVE:** Vehicles in the training park including T681, RF392 and an unidentified DMS, to the right is uniform issue service vehicle 1992F which has replaced one of the former BEA 1½ deck AEC Regals, note the height to allow people to stand upright inside for uniform fitting. **2 July 1983**

**ABOVE:** Cable drum carrier, service vehicle 2389L, in the lorry park at Chiswick works. **2 July 1983**

**ABOVE:** Distilled water carrier service vehicle 2394F in the lorry park at Chiswick works. **2 July 1983**

**BELOW**: During the Gala open day RT786 and DMO3 were giving rides to local underground stations seen here inside the works. **2 July 1983**

**ABOVE:** Also repainted into '1933' livery was LS194 shown here during the open day. **2 July 1983**

**BELOW:** Leyland National LS402 from Harrow Weald garage was painted into 'Jubilee' livery as seen here amongst the crowds of visitors on Gala day. **2 July 1983**

**LEFT:** Seen here in the experimental shop Leyland Titan T684 has been fitted with Voith transmission in place of the original Leyland Hydrocyclic unit. **2 July 1983**

**BELOW:** The first two Routemasters RM1 and RM2 form part of a line up at the Gala day. **2 July 1983**

**ABOVE:** The complete line of Routemasters at the Gala day, the intention had been to get RMs1, 2, 3, RMC4, RMs 5, 6, 7 & 8 plus FRM1(at the far end of the line). Unfortunately RM5 was unfit and a substitute was sent, which didn't get past enthusiast scrutiny on the day. **2 July 1983**

**BELOW:** Fake RM5 plus RMs 6 to 8 and FRM1 at the Gala day at Chiswick works, RM8 was one of the vehicles repainted into '1933' livery. **2 July 1983**

**ABOVE:** RMs 6, 7 & 8 at the Gala day. **2 July 1983**

**BELOW:** A line of vehicles in the Chiswick 'dip', training bus DMS2168 stands at the back of the line. **2 July 1983**

**ABOVE:** New Metrobus M877 parked in the Chiswick 'dip'. **2 July 1983**

**BELOW:** New Leyland Titan T790 leads the other vehicles parked in the Chiswick 'dip'. **2 July 1983**

**ABOVE:** Titan T789 is being used to demonstrate the use of mobile vehicle hoists at the Gala day. **2 July 1983**

**BELOW:** Metrobus M876 is similarly raised by mobile hoists. **2 July 1983**

**ABOVE:** DMS Fleetline D2629 was painted into this 'Chocolate Box' livery to mark the anniversary of Croydon Corporation Tramways in 1983. **2 July 1983**

**BELOW:** Voith transmissions were using former MBA458 to promote their products and fitted this bus with a Voith transmission. **2 July 1983**

**ABOVE:** Two more vehicles seen here specially painted to mark the 50th anniversary of London Transport were T747 into a gold livery (and re-numbered T1983) and DMS1933 in '1933' livery. **2 July 1983**

**BELOW:** Metrobus M57 was outshopped from Aldenham in this smart 'general' livery. **2 July 1983**

**ABOVE:** New as SMS91 the former SMD91 became the Video-bus with a livery to suit. **2 July 1983**

**BELOW:** Yet to enter service new Metrobus M809 shows its engine and transmission during the Gala day. **2 July 1983**

**LEFT:** The second day of the Gala weekend and this is RM1037 the West Ham garage showbus specially painted and restored as seen here, although unfortunately it was not parked in a place for easy photographs. **3 July 1983**

**BELOW:** RM2116 was painted in '1933' livery which it still carries today in preserved private ownership. The only Routemaster painted gold was appropriately RM1983 as seen here. **3 July 1983**

**ABOVE:** Metrobus M1 is on display, of particular note is its black skirt and different front destination blind box from the production vehicles (M6 onwards). **3 July 1983**

**BELOW:** Bertie the bus former RF 479 is used for charity work seen here surrounded by happy children. **3 July 1983**

# Another Day Another Skid

On the second day the two skid buses RT1530 and RMC1518 gave special displays without passengers, here they are both seen during the displays. **3 July 1983**

**ABOVE:** The 1984 open day and brand new T1050 hoisted on jacks is allowing visitors to inspect its underside. **5 August 1984**

**BELOW:** Training bus DMS1479 allocated to Potters Bar garage heads a line of buses at the Chiswick 'dip'. **5 August 1984**

**ABOVE:** Restored Service vehicle 1282F on display during the open day. **5 August 1984**

**BELOW:** MD1 has returned to Chiswick works now being owned by dealer Brakell with advertising for his business on the front upper side panels. **5 August 1984**

**ABOVE:** Former West Midlands Leyland Titan WDA5T has become LT T1130. **5 August 1984**

**LEFT:** RM1414 had been used as a demonstrator in Manchester during early 1963 and when sold in 1982 was acquired by the Museum of Transport in that city. It has made a return to London especially for this event. **5 August 1984**

**ABOVE:** Two DMS fleetlines in special liveries, DMS2629 to celebrate Croydon Corporation Tramways and DMS1933 retains its 1933 livery that it received the previous year, adverts showing that it had recently been used on the shuttle service to the annual Wimbledon Lawn Tennis Championships. **5 August 1984**

**BELOW:** Minibus Ford Transit FS22 on display with blinds for the Potters Bar local service PB1 which required just one vehicle. **5 August 1984**

**ABOVE:** DMS1515 was being used to advertise the righting of a fallen vehicle (next display at 1530pm), fortunately it was not this bus that was turned over. Several years later this bus would later become 'Supercar' to advertise travelcards – a ticket that was accepted on buses, tubes and trains in the London area. In this guise it still exists in private ownership in 2006. **5 August 1984**

**BELOW:** Red Arrow Mark II Leyland National LS448 leaves Chiswick works. The black bumpers were an unusual feature at the time. **5 August 1984**

**ABOVE:** The unique Volvo Ailsa V3 on display. The front mounted engine allowed doors to be fitted at both front and rear of the bus as can be seen here. Despite being severely damaged when it 'fell over' while operating at Potters Bar it has survived and was extensively restored by Black Prince near Leeds, it is now back in the London area and the rear door is to be re-instated soon. **5 August 1984**

**BELOW:** Training bus DMS1833 allocated to Holloway (HT) garage on display during the open day. **5 August 1984**

**ABOVE:** DMS1967 was converted into a 'radio training bus' for the BUSCO system hence additional aerials housed under domes on the roof, seen here at the Chiswick 'dip' looking in remarkably good condition. This bus survives as a promotional bus in Europe in 2006. **5 August 1984**

**BELOW:** Former DMS264 was now in the ownership of Ensignbus and re-numbered DMO264 to reflect its open top form and use on the Round London Sightseeing Tour. **5 August 1984**

**ABOVE:** Metrobus M205 has been allocated to the experimental shop at Chiswick where it is seen with a new Deutz air cooled engine fitted. **5 August 1984**

**LEFT:** DMS2034 seen on display with unusual yellow paint around its upper deck windows in place of the usual white. **5 August 1984**

OUC 34 R

**ABOVE:** Two sold Routemasters with new owners on display. RCL2254 is now with Bonay services Ltd as a staff bus and open top RM1403 with Ind Coope Ltd carrying Benskins brewery. **5 August 1984**

**BELOW:** Former West Midlands Leyland Titan WDA2T is now fitted with coach seats, numbered T1127 and in use by Selkent Travel for private hire work, alongside is DM2643 which is used for similar work. **5 August 1984**

**ABOVE:** RML2402 has gained yellow bands to emphasise its use on route 15, alongside is the last production Routemaster RML2760 with its original flake grey centre band. **5 August 1984**

**BELOW:** Three more Routemasters on display, on the left is BEA Routemaster No.54, then grey BEL Ltd liveried RMA16 and finally Northern General Routemaster 2095. **5 August 1984**

**ABOVE:** Metrobus M1104 was one of a batch allocated to Brixton garage fitted from new with the Cummins L10 engine seen here on display with appropriate side advertising for the engine manufacturer and a Cummins badge on the front grill. **5 August 1984**

**BELOW:** London Country were displaying their latest Green Line coach STL2 from Dunton Green garage a far cry from a previous generation of STLs. **5 August 1984**